Contents

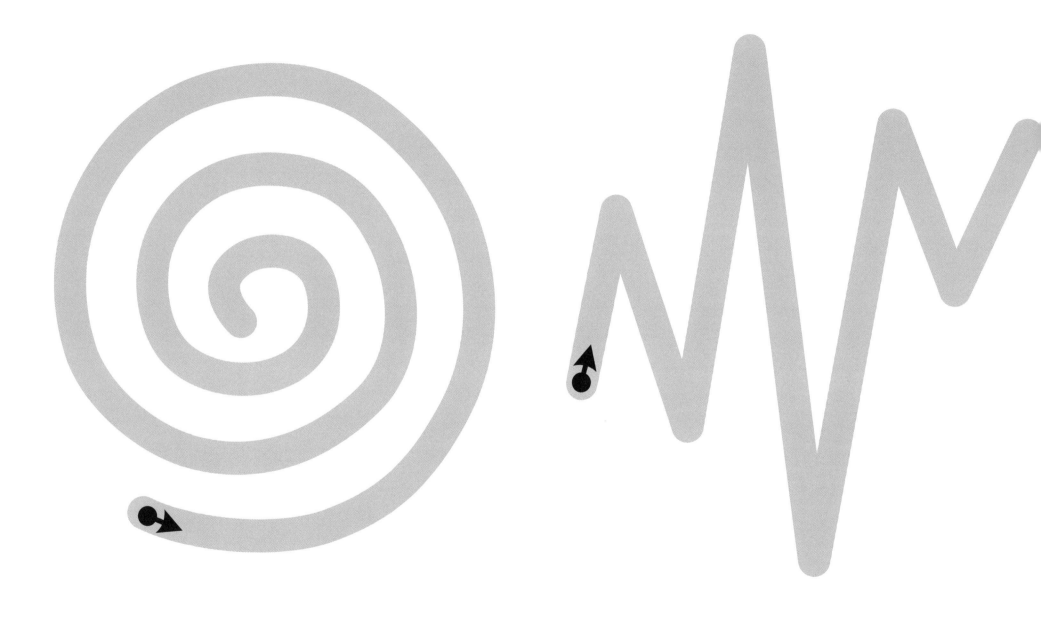

Hello
Shape awareness

1 Trace with your finger.　　**2** Trace with a crayon.　　**3** Say the color.

Vocabulary: Colors

Structure: What color is it?

1 **Look and find.**   2 **Trace the circles with a crayon.**

Vocabulary: circle, boy, girl, ball

Structure: It's a (circle).

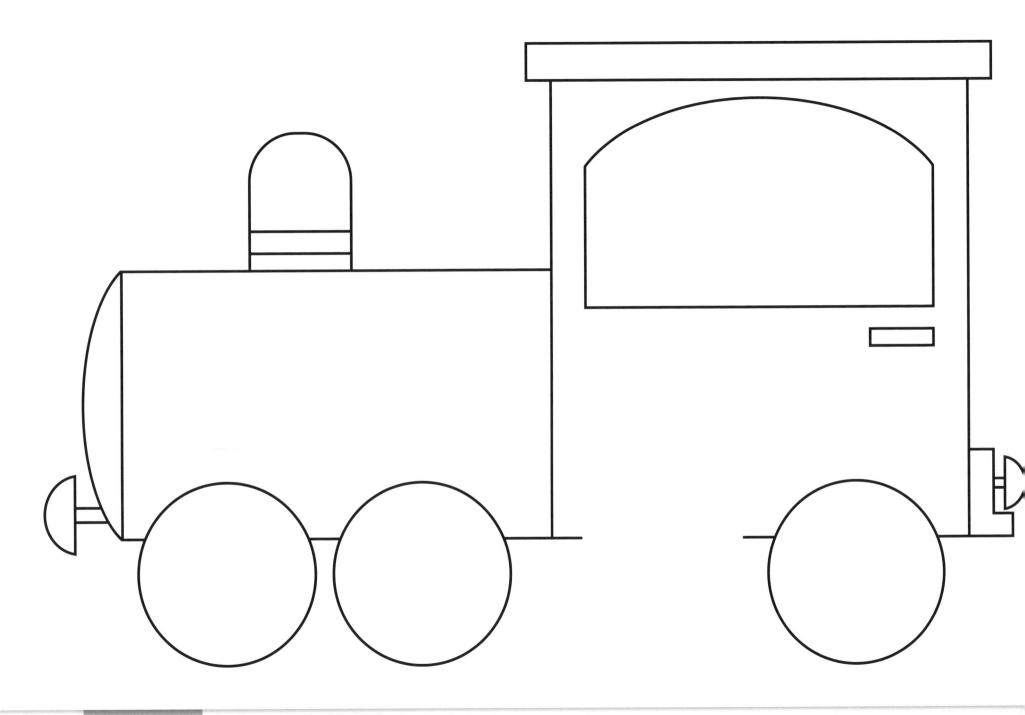

Unit 1
Recognizing the need
for a shape

1 **Look.**   2 **What's missing?**   3 **Draw.**
Vocabulary: **1, wheel,** train
Structure: It's a train.

1 Count.   2 Draw snowballs.   3 Color.
Vocabulary: 1, 2, snowballs

Unit 1
Spatial awareness
First/last

1 Color the first person blue.   **2** Color the last person red.   **3** Say.

Vocabulary: **first, last,** mom, brother, sister, dad

Structure: Who's (first)?

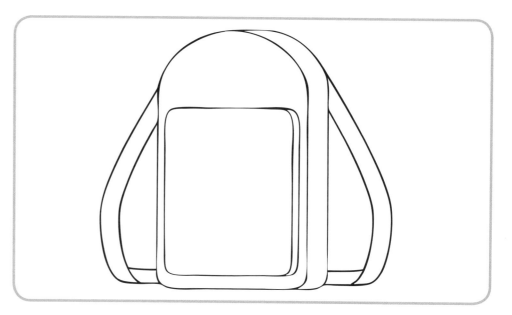

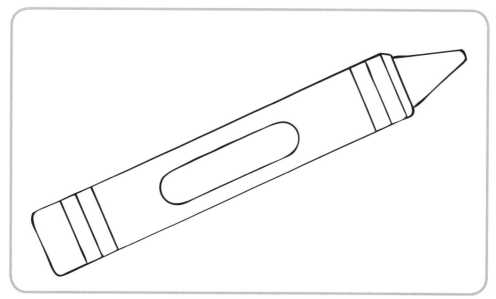

1 Count.   **2 Color if there is 1.**   **3 Close your book and remember.**

Vocabulary: 1, 2, books, bag, crayon,

Structure: How many (books) are there?

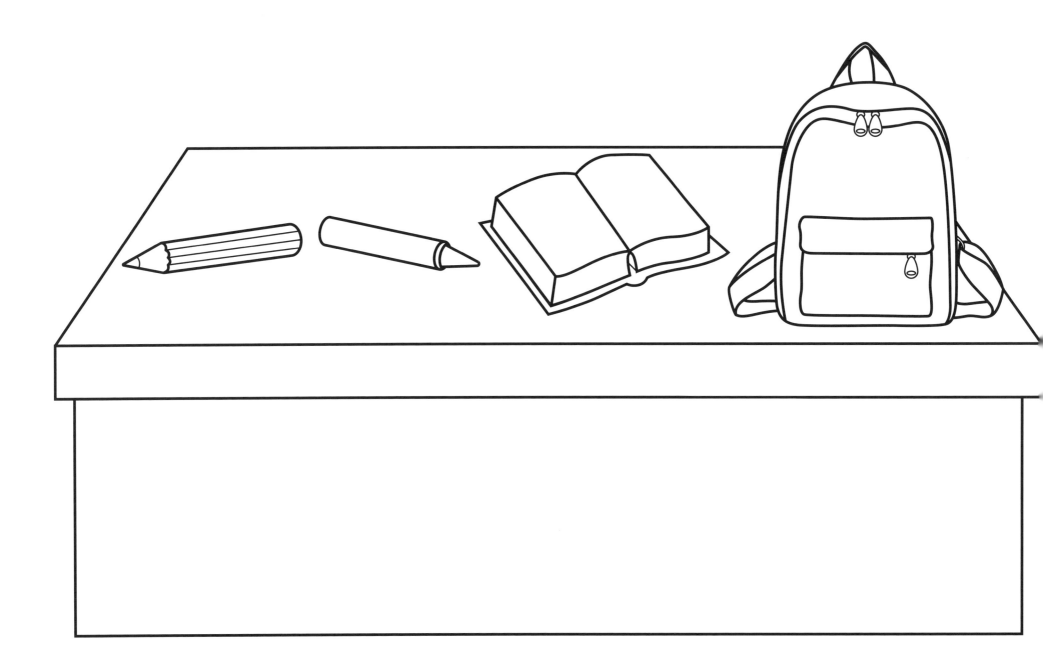

Unit 2
Revision of first/last

1 What's this?   **2 Say the first and color.**   **3 Say the last and color.**

Vocabulary: pencil, crayon, book, bag, first, last, Colors
Structures: What's this?   What color is the (pencil)?

1 **Look and trace with your finger.**   2 **Match with number flashcards.**   3 **Color.**

Vocabulary: 1, 2, **stick, swan**

Structure: What's this?

1 **What's in your box?**   2 **Count.**   3 **Say.**

Vocabulary: 1, 2, **3**, **4**, **cars**, boats, balls, cat

Structures: **What's in your box?**   **How many (boats) are there?**   **(2) (boats).**

1 **Count.** 2 **Draw the same number of dots.**

Vocabulary: 1,2, eyes, ears, nose, mouth

Structures: How many (eyes)? (2) (eyes).

Unit 3
Counting and matching
objects to dots

11

Unit 3
Counting to 2

1 Trace.   2 Color.   3 Count and say.

Vocabulary: 1, 2, boy, girl, eyes, ears, nose, mouth

Structure: How many (ears)?

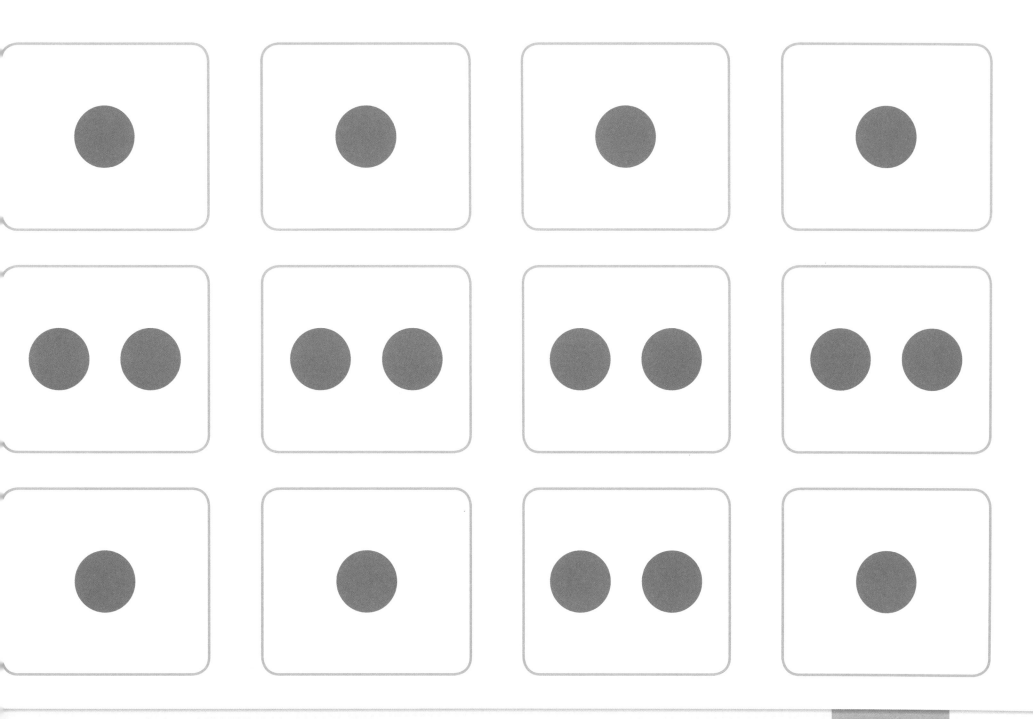

1 Look.   **2 Count the dots.**   **3 Clap the number and say.**

Vocabulary: 1, 2, **clap**

Structure: How many dots?

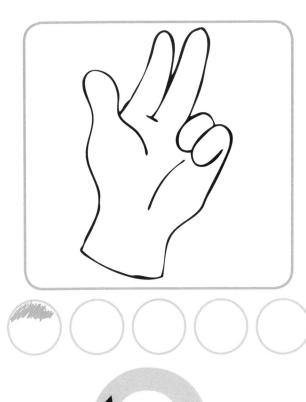

Unit 3
Counting to 5
Numbers 3–5

1 **Count the fingers.**　　2 **Color.**　　3 **Trace.**

Vocabulary:　3, 4, **5**, fingers

Structures:　How many fingers?　(3) fingers.

1 **Look and say.**   2 **Look and trace the windows.**   3 **Color.**

Vocabulary: **windows, square,** bus

Structures: What's this?   How many windows are there?

Unit 4
Recognizing similar
shapes

1 **Look and trace.** 2 **Find and trace.** 3 **Color.**

Vocabulary: square, window, bus, train

Structures: What's this? A (train).

1 Point and draw dots.   **2 Color the first.**   **3 Color the last.**

Vocabulary: 1, 2, 3, 4, first, last

Structure: How many dots are there?

Unit 4
Recognizing shapes
Counting to 5

1 Count the shapes.   **2** Count the dots.   **3** Match.
Vocabulary: 1–5, bus, windows, wheels, circle, square
Structure: How many (windows)?

1 Look and count.   2 Color.   3 Say.

Vocabulary: flowers, bees, trees, **more**, **fewer**

Structure: How many (flowers)?

Unit 5
Estimation of objects
to 5

1 Count. **2 Color if there are 5** . **3 Close your book and remember.**

Vocabulary: 1–5, flowers, bees, tree

Structure: How many (flowers)?

1 Look and point. **2** Color if it is bigger. **3** Say.

Vocabulary: small, smaller, big, bigger, Prickly, Benny, tree

Structures: Is he/she (smaller)? Is this (bigger)?

Unit 5
Identifying the same
number of items 1–6

1 Look at the flower and count the petals.   **2 Count.**   **3 Color if it is the same.**

Vocabulary: 1–5, **6**, petals, flowers

Structure: How many petals?

1 Look and count.   2 Color if there are more.   3 Say.

Vocabulary: 7, 1–6, trains, cars, balls, more, fewer

Structure: How many (trains)?

Unit 6
Identifying picture
differences

1 Look, point, and say.   **2 Find the differences.**   **3 Say.**

Vocabulary: toy box, table, chair, train, computer, hat, on, in
Structures: Where's (the computer)?   (In) the (toy box).

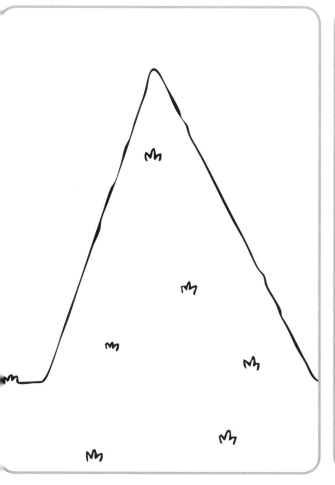

1 Find.   **2 Color.**   **3 Say.**

Vocabulary: triangle, **star,** hill, hat, boy, toy box

Structures: Where's a (triangle)?   How many (stars)?

Unit 6
Counting to 9

1 Count the △. **2** Count the □. **3** Color if there are more.

Vocabulary: **8, 9,** 1–7, mat, triangles, squares

Structure: How many (squares)?

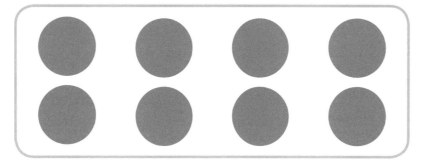

1 Count the dots.   **2 Count the pets.**   **3 Color if there are the same.**

Vocabulary: 1–8, cats, turtles, **the same**

Structure: How many (cats)?

Unit 7
Counting to 9
Identifying the same

1 Match.   2 Count.   3 Say.

Vocabulary: 9, 1–8, cats, balls

Structures: How many (cats)?   9 (cats).

1 Look and point.　**2** Count.　**3** Draw the spots.

Vocabulary:　dog, **spots,** the same

Structure:　How many (spots)?

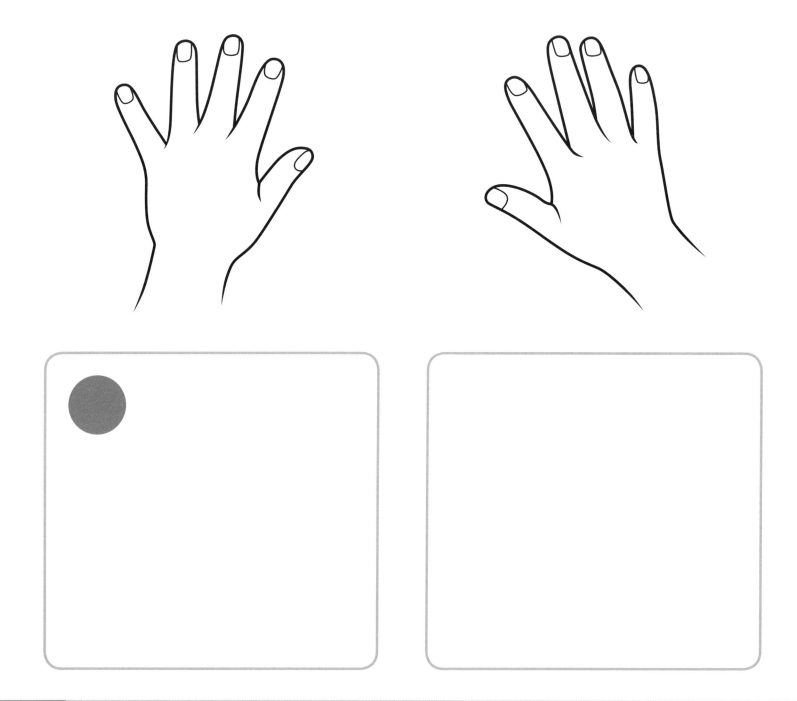

Unit 7
Counting to 10
The same

1 Look.   **2 Count.**   **3 Draw the dots.**
Vocabulary: **10**, 5, 1–9, fingers, dots
Structure: How many (fingers)?

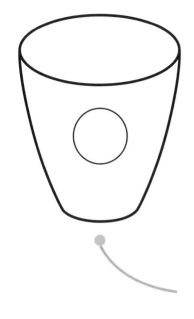

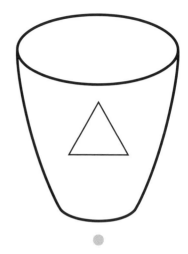

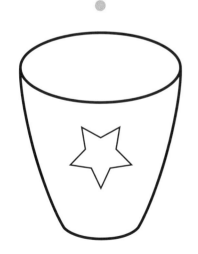

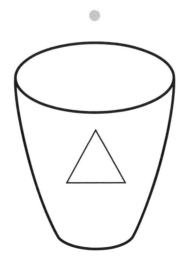

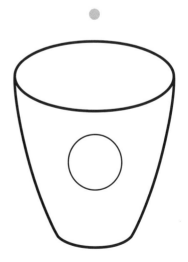

1 Look and point.   2 Match.   3 Say.

Vocabulary: 1–6, cups, circles, stars, triangles, the same

Structure: Is it the same?

Unit 8
More/fewer
Preparing for addition

1 Look and count.   2 Color where there are more.

Vocabulary: 1–10, **stack**, cups

Structure: Who can stack more cups?

1 Count. 2 Draw fewer bubbles in picture 2. 3 Count and say.

Vocabulary: bubbles, more, fewer

Structure: How many bubbles?

Unit 8
Counting 1–10
Preparing for addition

1 Match.   **2** What's missing?   **3** Draw.

Vocabulary: 1–10, children, cups, **one more**

Structures: How many (children/cups)?   What's missing?

1 Look and say.   2 What's next?   3 Draw.
Vocabulary: grapes, apple, banana, strawberry
Structure: What's next?

Unit 9
Identifying the same
number of items in sets

1 Look and count the grapes.   **2 Circle if it is the same.**   **3 Say.**

Vocabulary: 1–10, grapes, the same

Structures: How many (grapes)?   Is it the same?

1 **Look and count.**   2 **Share and draw.**   3 **Say.**

Vocabulary: 1–4, **share**, cookies
Structure: How many (cookies)?

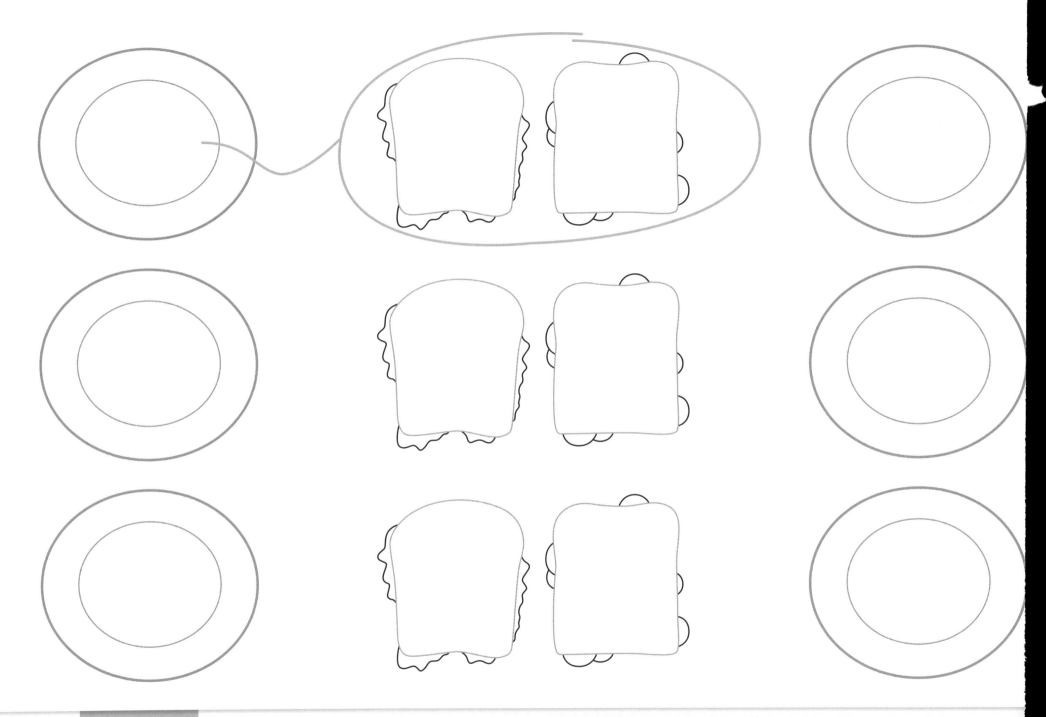

Unit 9 Sorting two items in different ways

1 Look and sort the sandwiches in different ways.　**2** Trace.　**3** Circle and draw a line.

Vocabulary: 1–2, sandwiches, plate

Structure: How many (sandwiches)?

1 Look and point.   2 Match.   3 Say.

Vocabulary: pet, toy, bird, mouse, cat, turtle, boat, ball, teddy bear, car

Structures: What's this?   It's a (pet/toy).

Review 2

Spatial awareness

1 Trace with your finger.   **2** Trace with a crayon.   **3** Say.

Vocabulary: girl, boy, banana, strawberries, apples, sandwich

Structure: What snack does (the boy/girl) like?